CHROMATIC

Also by H. L. Hix

POETRY
Shadows of Houses*
Surely As Birds Fly
Rational Numbers
Perfect Hell

ARTISTS' BOOKS AND LIMITED EDITIONS
This Translucent Tissue *(artist's book by Judi Ross)*
The Last Hour *(artist's book by Egidijus Rudinskas)*
Intellectual Pleasures *(limited edition by Aralia Press)*

TRANSLATION
On the Way Home,
trans. with Jüri Talvet
A Call for Cultural Symbiosis,
by Jüri Talvet, trans. with the author
City of Ash,
by Eugenijus Ališanka, trans. with the author

ARTIST CATALOGS
Jason Pollen
Kyoung Ae Cho

THEORY AND CRITICISM
Wild and Whirling Words: A Poetic Conversation*
As Easy As Lying: Essays on Poetry *
Understanding William H. Gass
Understanding W. S. Merwin
Spirits Hovering Over the Ashes:
Legacies of Postmodern Theory
Morte d'Author: An Autopsy

*Also published by Etruscan Press

CHROMATIC

H. L. Hix

etruscan press

Etruscan Press
Graduate Creative Writing Program
Wilkes University
82 West South Street
Wilkes-Barre, PA 18766

www.etruscanpress.org

Publisher's Cataloging-in-Publication
(Provided by Quality Books, Inc.)

    Hix, H. L.
        Chromatic / H.L. Hix.
        p. cm.
        Poems.
        ISBN 0-9745995-6-5

        I. Title.

    PS3558.I88C57 2006   811'.54
                     QBI06-600126

Designed by Elizabeth Woll

The publication of Chromatic has been made possible by
grants from the National Endowment for the Arts and
the Ohio Arts Council.

Acknowledgments

Some of these poems enjoyed journal publication, for which I thank the editors of *Angle, Denver Quarterly, Northwest Review, Ploughshares, Pool,* and *Practice.*

I owe particular thanks to Warren Rosser and Stephen Burt for their promptings.

The epigraphs, in order of their appearance, are from:
Baruch Spinoza, *Ethics*
W. G. Sebald, *Austerlitz*
Ludwig Wittgenstein, *Remarks on Colour*
Emmanuel Levinas, *God, Death, and Time*
J. S. Bach, title page of *The Well-Tempered Clavier*

Table of Contents

Desire is the very nature or essence of every single individual.

•

I feel more and more as if time did not exist at all, only various spaces interlocking according to the rules of a higher form of stereometry, between which the living and the dead can move back and forth as they like, and the longer I think about it the more it seems to me that we who are still alive are unreal in the eyes of the dead, that only occasionally, in certain lights and atmospheric conditions, do we appear in their field of vision. As far back as I can remember, . . . I have always felt as if I had no place in reality, as if I were not there at all.

Remarks on Color

How must we look at this problem in order for it to become solvable?

•

Boy meets girl, girl smiles.
Boy colors and looks down.

I see music, a colored medium
that darkens its surroundings.

Her bright body the iris,
his dark mind the pupil.

He hears the night as dark,
she hears it as a medium.

•

Red-brown in daybreak's red-brown light
a dolor of doves pavanes on the lawn
under these capricious trees,
but here color loves the evening,
always and only in secret,
withdrawn, watching from a distance
a brazen taint of starlings
brag its black advances.

•

Walking in the woods alone,
holding a lantern, stepping carefully,
abstracting everything, looking for you —
a color shines in darkness —
I passed a pond. Three men
stopped fishing to chase me
and I ran and ran and ran
but my fear was for you.

•

After first shy fascination becomes
the primordial relationship,
position, look at your room

late in mathematics
in asymptotic light.
A human form will appear
when you can hardly see color,
when the rules decide they want you.

•

Doesn't white erase importance?

How important can one glance be?

A glance can be stolen, but from whom?

Stolen fire burns hottest.

Windburn, sunburn, snowblindness.

Blind singer's song, blind woman's touch.

Close your eyes and touch me there.

Am I the broad line your touch erases?

•

I wanted to smudge you my number
but could dream no pen, no paper.
Here we sleep a question of color,
we who want, we who veil.
You were backing slowly away,
slurring into someone else.
I knew you would not return.
I knew you, but not myself.

•

What feeling inhabits the concept
of saturated color?

What names the crease
behind your knees? the skin on your knuckles?

the way my hand rests on your waist
when you lie on your side?

the whorls at the small of your back?
Can we say what surrounds us now?

•

Whiter love provokes brighter lusts.
Do you know what 'reddish' means?
On your body? On someone else's?
Is it better not to know?
Can you find it on me?
Where else have you looked?
Should I apply to the stars
what you told me of the moon?

•

Blue obliterates yellow.
The moon replaces the sun.
Winter makes even the stars cold.
Blue requires opposition.

I fell in love with the cold you,
your blue planets restless
among your cold blue stars,
each seeking perfect isolation.

•

He calls love the abstraction that counts.
She says love is no abstraction.

He asks how it would help to know
a direct route blue to yellow.
She hums the subject retrograde.

He thinks what he feels may be love.
She feels no need to think.

Portraits are landscapes, more or less veiled.

•

Felled, shredded, soaked to paper,
screened, sedimented, felted, layered
by your knowing hands that left
the colors kinship and daydown,
that purified duality,
I fell in love with the ways I might die,
the elements that might consume me,
earth, water, fire, you.

•

When we love we love color,
the closing and confusion of our gaze
by something inexplicable.

Cloudiness cannot tell red from green
and knows better than to try.

My love for you assumes
either the color of sawdust,
or of a milk snake's shed skin.

•

I lose luminosity
whenever I dream of you
and I always dream of you
though colors surface as causes
and causes submerge me
so I can't reach the surface
whose sun-conscious radiation
charges my dream-colored drowning.

●

In bright life we surrender
to ravenous colors:
the oily sheen of beetles' backs
leaving a deer's eye sockets,
your aura when you touch
the circle of darkened fur
outlining its open belly
and turn to look back at me.

●

Don't forget that transparency
and gray can both be painted,
though not with transparent paint.
Don't forget that as years get shorter
love matters more, the lover matters less,
that the palpable can be abstract,
that you can lie about love
to your lover, or to yourself.

●

What makes bright colors different?
He says one thing, she says another.

How does saturation feel?
He thinks he knows, she thinks he doesn't.

Why does one color's advance
return the others to broad contour?

He thinks it is not one color.
She thinks the other colors merge.

●

Don't tell me there is no such thing
as luminous properties.
I feel them when I close my eyes,

when my hands, alive through light, wander
over your shoulders, your neck,
across your belly, behind your knees,
down your forearm elbow to wrist.
Your ankles glow, your shoulderblades shine.

•

I couldn't understand
how you could laugh underwater
or why you kept pulling me down.
The implied, we see abstractly.
Colors have qualities and effects.
You were a vivid yellow-green.
Or she was who looked like you
in the boat, just out of my reach.

•

When you are gone, at night in my room
the particular falls away
and objects of luminous colors,
opalescent jellyfish
a mile below the surface,
drift, abstract in the cold current,
viscous stars thrown off
by a dissolving galaxy.

•

Confined so long in one frame,
me mocking your movements you mocking mine,
we organized our environment
into the story color told us,

the story of definite darkness,
brownian movement, expanding space,
suns burned out before our birth,
dancing and dancing till closing time.

•

Love means the soul only pivots.
Any name can be erased.

I knew it would before it did.
This visible life conceals others.

Line and color are general truths.
A dark red can be blue too.

What I say of someone else
hues itself true of you.

•

My hands that once called forth color
now tighten to a fetal fist.
No more cello, no more rocks
rounded by rivers, warmed by the sun,
no more tautening to the absolute,
touching one of your nipples
with my outstretched ring finger
and the other with my thumb.

•

These oblongs of light I take
as a message, you as a messenger.
I watch you. I hear what you say
and how you say it, your compulsion
to express the absolute.
Is red lighter than yellow?
I don't know. I resonate
at the pitch your tautness tells me to.

•

Your life looms over my life.

I hear you, but I can't find you.

Everything I made I made as gifts.

Do we share the same emotion?

I watch for your visit, bird.

When you go, leave me your shadow.

The shadow white casts is gray.

Sometimes I can't tell which one is you.

•

I may be introverted but.

There are different definitions of.

I always wanted to with.

Additionally the light.

If only I had listened when.

Long ago I gave up trying to.

No one who says that of pure colors.

When we are I imagine you as.

•

The grade is imperceptible
but enough to slow the train
even after what you did to me.
What did you not do to me?

Which is odder: to say brown is solid,
or that you love only me?

One color exists through another.
The ice melted, but froze again.

•

Because the stars knew snow was coming
and that our firewood could not last
I was frantic to show you
I could pass through walls
and that white cancels all reflection
but ice formed inside the windows
and you cried knowing my fetching wood
left only the two of you.

•

If we get in trouble it's your fault.
That we haven't yet is mine.

Why do I never fulfill
desires as simple as these?

Shape, movement, a little color,
our inner tragic pushing order out.

I mean more than I can say aloud.
Why is there no gray light?

•

I was on fire but what scared me
was that all I touched began to burn,
the tragic made material,
light licked from my luminous hand,
and I backed away from your approach,
throwing down books to slow you
but you ate them and their flames
shone yellow-green in your eyes.

•

Floured palms dimpling dough,
one pair of lips against another,
ice melting off branches onto snow,
ice shaping rock for a million years.

Now I see the abstract.
I feel the impression of color,
the hole a rootball leaves
when a leaning life falls.

•

Try to paint what you see
when you see through my eyes
as once I wanted to see through yours.
I want now only to remember
color purely seen, looking into them,
watching from outside at night
two women in a lighted room
drinking rum and laughing.

•

In place of lesser abstractions
I wonder now only about love,
about how to paint this graying light,
how to look at this darkening
and say what it reminds me of,
or who it calls to mind,
beautiful but never touched,
who was with me once, or might have been.

Eighteen Maniacs

A hunger that no music appeases.

Please Say You Will

Voodoo | Dream do the rain or am I drink it? Keep secret your sun-squinted hues. Deeper disclosures drain down spilled colors clouds couldn't kept.

Felicity | One earring same size as your world mind-wide from one same size as mine.

Stoptime | Gone mother underground gone somewhere else, gone measure, gone melody.

Syphilis | Smaller bear-brother, caught kin, marked one, meander of tracks memorial in morning mud.

Peacherine | You'd laugh if I tolja.

Treemonisha | I know just what you means.

Swipesy | When I looked up, the back window was black that watched the woods that had been purple-green, deer-dark, dimly stippled before I looked down.

Rabbit Foot

Will | Change key. Will not bigword you you
don't barnyard me. Will wax no more. My
songmoon no record wane mine not yours.

Shack | You see it out there I hear it in here sure. Leaf-
listings and frost-shimmy, sun gone cold, gone
south. Gun-gray geese, those blood-drawn
veerings that out-grace grace.

Ma | Always one woman keep drawin up buckets.
Spill make stones darkshine, make mud. Rope
water up. Big she bend strong back down.
Wide feet, wide whatnot. Always water there,
always more, always plenty.

Lovie | Need no slow ocean. Spill past, cold-over
one. Froth up food for slim-slick trout. Down
outloves level.

Nix | Not slick enough'll stop that. No spill today,
nat means no spill never. Short sell hustle me
undone. Should've held, should've held.

Countin' | Sugar maple, shadbush, sycamore, sassafrass,
shagbark, rose of sharon.

Shake It

Nigger #2	|	Believe you then neither.
Sporting house	|	Hard-coded, what we're showin you is. Sing out, show out, hack access down three sold-over regions.
Papa mutt	|	Don't think so.
Grandpa's spells	|	Shouldna mowed no lawn, notnee's at old, notna sun's so hot. Shoulda stayed inside. Missed him he stepped out. Miss him now.
Mamanita	|	No more knock-kneed noise once we roll around. Call down carpet burn. Come on.
Pearls	|	Knot tween each mean only one roll off lost when the got-to get him hurry-up clumsy.
Crave	|	Circle the house while I sleep. Feel no need to speak. Like dark cold cloudshine. Know everything upwind.
Deep creek	|	Go slow. Deep creek call out all over, gather brown all falldown all riseup. Deep creek kiss river, give all over, level down to no bounds gone green water.

Emergency

Selma | Traded my weather for Deetroit weather. Cold snap come sometime I know, come some big snow. No point front porch, smoke smell outsell sweat. Sing inside, time come for me to.

Big | Omigod.

Downhearted | Took two t-shirts, done my ten days' time. Wash dishes all the yelled-at night, eat the leavins, you'd take t-shirts too.

Jailhouse | Had one window wouldn't mind. Nobody free miss me, but don't I miss the sun. New name some days. Selma most. Sweet Selma.

Lost your head | Same time I lost mine. Lose it again next you.

City blues | Miss oakshade cool. Snow here make no mud. Miss bramblescars, tickitches. Miss mushrooms. Miss pickin burrs off socks. Miss meet me deershy in the clearing. Miss no cars no trains sweet owlcall sleep.

Darling | We woan do nothin you doan wanna.

I've Found a New Baby

Ja Da	|	Everybody wanna see Paris once. Everybody love to learn a new song.
Logic	|	Follow south some attribute south of god modified by some twist made infinite through that same south attribute come north necessarily and infinitely.
Limehouse	|	Modest place, that place we go. Course shade cover it cool. Course the browned down pine quills quilt it soft. Course that spring still colds on up there.
Wild cat	|	Stay too long mean not really there. Not there now musta never been.
Cake walkin' babies	|	Sing barbershop, sing bow tie and striped shirt and straw, sing because. Because straw man strung down, strung out, strung together, because you know why. No rocket scientist. Why I sing, why I stop. Because you *are* why. Sing down that striped shirt, sing off those soft shoes, that bass sweeping up slow those sweet lines that tenor left swift behind.
Shag	|	Then dyin again to make sure.

I Can Study Rain

Delta | Last year drop down clay this year spread out water. Start out snow turn orchids here.

Twenty-nine songs | Buckets from a well drilled down to hell. No, spills sloshed from buckets. No, mud made by spills. No, what seeps through mud all the way down.

Low-down achin' | *She want fifty cents and I lacks a nickel.*

Me and the devil | First deal I struck a real winner. You. That done down one mouth moment for all the rest.

Passway | Two good eyes, but don't do dark. Don't do this tunnel under ash mountain. Seem long, seem oughta be out now, oughta be light. Still walk, still cold, still down. No turnin back, just as dark behind. I hear her cryin, a ways back or a ways ahead. Can't tell. Two good ears, but hear the same thing all the time. Two good legs go forward find more cold more wet. Light gone out long time back. This love note scrawled in the dark left for anybody crawl down this far got fingers good enough to feel what it whisper.

Hellhound | Kennel anything long enough it'll howl at where the whittled earth drops off.

Two stepfathers | And can't but one give you your name.

Hot-foot powder | Cut feet sore. Got loud, got cold, got hot, got salt. Need no more for dancin. But you. Or what I still got, the thought of you.

Ramblin' | Places I been ain't missed much but seen no white squirrels like you got here.

Shines | One-line sun love this lake run one finger up her back mornin down again night.

Prelude to a Kiss

Bubber | Get down train some town you know nobody, nothin for when you walk but whistle.

Plug | Powder cap, carbon cushion, yellow-footed chantarelle, imperial cat, blood-red cort, pestle-shaped coral, cystoderma, corpse finder.

Aunt Tillie | Liked the phrase *vaguely sinful,* lived like it was meant for her.

Hot and sweet | What exactly could a lover write on those last postcards from the edge of the world, why can only singing bring her back through expanding black? Is there light except stars at the rim of this blasted universe, calling back to our sad bright planet?

Chalumeau | What if I don't draw this landscape in a certain light at one moment from one station? What if instead of placing others in it I move through it myself? What if I see it as numbers, as sequence, as something that erases me, proof not that I was here but that I never existed, and could not possibly? What if I don't see this landscape at all, but hear it in my head singing swingingly?

Cootie | Sometimes anger at the start, always sorrow in the end.

Cup-muted | Later, baby. Not now. Not right now.

Blue serge | Dress up gone to see you.

Mood indigo | Love has felt like falling asleep in snow,
knowing, not choosing exactly but not
resisting either, fascinated by this cold cold
light bent blue.

Dusk | Why not love coming-on dark? Bats sing
their way through this world.

Misbehavin'

Gully low | Maybe god speak off mountains too, but my muddy Moses brung up tablets from one brown down ditch. 1. Start small. 2. Meander. 3. Indiscriminate is good; accept everything. 4. Carry it with you. 5. Carry it all with you. 6. Swell; flood. 7. Stop for no one. 8. Look back at mountains, forward to the sea. 9. Patience rubs rocks round; brown water washes white things clean. 10. Ascend and start over.

Sweet mama | First thing she did was laugh. I knew first thing.

Storyville | Trouble how much time you got when no one loves you.

Waifs | Can't find it on the streets don't need it.

Roseland | World I breathe need none better to back it up or come along after. Look pretty, smell good. It. You.

Lil | Diplodon, dosinia, donax, drupe, distorsio, drillia, dogwinkle, dwarf triton.

Gut bucket | Small disaster mean minor mercy.

Hotter than that | Less you can do about it, longer it takes to happen. First thing I saw, her eyes giving back light when she lifted her head. I knew she would bolt, I knew

I was going too fast, I knew her fawn
would follow. She could've gotten past,
but it was like she stopped, like that
was how she wanted both of us to die,
her by my headlights, me by her body.
Never mind I can tell you this. Doesn't
mean she didn't get her wish.

Lyin' to myself | Can't sing what you can turn away from.

Sure Thing

Five by five	|	Followed you here. Why not? What else? Nothing not you matters now. Yes I knew better. No I won't go.
Tickle Joe	|	Don't stop followin my eyes just cause they lie, won't stop followin my fingers.
Doggin'	|	Scaphoid, lunate, triquetral, pisiform, trapezium, trapezoid, capitate, hamate, metacarpals, phalanges.
Small hotel	|	I had an interesting childhood, I know these things. So when she started bawling I knew to stack yesterday's colors against the colors before. She wanted to hurt herself, I know about these things. I had a colored childhood. That's why they wear mascara, so you know they're crying. These things you learn after you hurt yourself, after they hurt you. I know a thing or two about stacking, about colors, about getting hurt, about the day before.
Stride	|	Left the bickering in the back room for the sure down shakin showin flesh out front. Sing no sad songs since.
Jumpin'	|	Happen when oughta-be-enough-for-now meet always-want-more.
'Way back	|	Starless night, dark deck, still sea, and the whales surfaced like she sent them, spouting in sequence as if for that one

startling moment she spoke through them before they dove again forever.

Cherry point | This one place we went to, being there made everything right. Night no darker there, stars no prettier, moon no bigger. No just-out-of-sight-waterfall sound silvered the air. We didn't talk more there. I didn't touch her. Didn't need to. Wanted nothing. Didn't gaze into her eyes. We didn't look at each other, just watched the world. Not that it came to us there, but that there — only there, only then — it had never gone away.

Swings the Band

Moonglow | *This* light.

Atlanta | The band was swingin and I only heard the gun in my one good ear.

Little joe | Taught me a man lose his color he fall hard down.

Zodiac | Heard the whole thing, but my eyes never *did* adjust.

Black christ | Which first said *save me,* she or he, neither knew. *If I kilned you in clay I would glaze you black.* She said. Or he did. *I am black, and have been always, though only your molding me so showed me the fact.* He said. Or she did. Either way, either way.

Rose | How many loves can name themselves? How many cruelties cannot?

Elfrieda | Wunna you boys rough-burl me some elbowed walnut first, then somebody spindle me up some sabled maple.

Mass | You call god proper think he sit on benches straight think he don't slouch think he try to echo think he home all that cold stone. Meantime I be playin lessee he don't come dance.

These Foolish Things

Can't get started | It ain't speakin to me I ain't speakin back.

Strange fruit | Didn't pass by many sins, wasn't gonna not taste you.

Funny that way | Wore-out run-down-to-mud same-way-every-time-I-let-her-out got-no-kind-of-sense one-corner-to-another-then-all-around-the-fence nose-down-like-she-could-catch-a-rabbit-anyway kind of path.

Drinkard | Falling-loud fountain's steady-hushed sound.

Tenderly | Him bein that old make me what? When he was a baby I rocked him a many a mile.

All of me | Can't give you what I never had myself.

44 | Come between me and you. Like everything else now. Telephone. Time zone. Feeble neighbors' lawns, overgrown. Get in line, 44, get in line.

Stormy weather | I told em wash her no more, her skin so thin. Walked back in she was bleedin, washed her skin right off.

Gotta right | To tell myself the truth while I lie to you. Gotta right to *try* to hear the snow.

Gotta right to wake up for sounds you
can't hear, then be afraid to fall back to
sleep. Gotta right to first-dime whisky,
second-dime bread. Gotta right to prefer
after to before. To hoard alibis. To end
with nothin if I started that way.

Palisades

Dizzy | Snow fuss a halo of the light, or light a halo of the snow?

Cheraw | Aspen she grow, more root than branch, earth-burrowed soul even when she shivers back the sun, one in all her risings, movin under me many seasons surround me now.

Shaw 'nuff | Them things shaw 'nuff purty. Touch em? Hold em? Gentle I be. Real gentle.

Quilombo | First field verify the floating walls then reclaim flexible space. Six throws of the hand shut it all down. Lose power to the core the code locks, three thousand kelvin knuckle and all. Fifty seats, static, find four floral columns staged to monitor a tricky world.

Nana | You can sing it it's one of my names.

Siboney | In my dream you still loved me. In my dream it had once been true that you did love me, not only that I wanted you to, so it was possible for you to love me still. Or at least it was possible for you to love me still despite your not having loved me before. Such is the logic of sleep, a logic I swallowed in my efforts to survive waking life. A bundle of wires insulated in bright colors, coiled into a sort of sleeve, sent off sparks when I put my arm in it. I think. Some parts of the dream felt uncertain, but that love was possible I remember clearly, so remarkable it seemed.

Caribe | Try to name what I want, I see you, I say this.

Well You Needn't

Round midnight | This dark she open the door light come in or go out?

Chaser | Small glass splinter look like a tiny fuse in my right index finger, pull it out not cause it hurt but to show off.

Epistrophy | Three minutes here, three minutes there, three take a life, three give one back, three minutes find a new baby, three minutes tell why, three say nothin don't need to, three minutes hang on, three minutes let go, three minutes your eyes close your arms around me sway, three minutes touch my wrist look in my eyes, three got to, three don't, three minutes always starting always done.

Misterioso | Somethin in me said same deflections left me outta your world showed me one of my own. Somethin in me said everything sing, said listen. Somethin in me said god work off by himself sometimes, don't say much. Somethin in me said stay home a year, nothin to hear can't hear in my head.

Bemsha | Flexor pollicis brevis, abductor digiti minimi, lumbrical, annular pulleys, cruciate pulleys.

Evidence | The answer. You are. That I am here. To my existence. On this planet.

Whose sun. Though I am alone.
When it explodes. I am here. Night
shimmers in the north. Answer. Me.

I mean you | Came right up in the yard they did,
quiet as you please, six of em together.
I was working on the shutters had my
back to em didn't know they were
there till I heard em chewing. Come
for fallen fruit under the pear tree they
had. I shifted on the ladder and they
all looked up together with those big
dark eyes like they were all one animal
but then they just went back to eating.
I watched em and thought they'd
stay longer but they walked off quick
as they came like they knew I'd see
nothin so beautiful ever again.

Melancholy Me

Scat | On the end got a hook some words do, down they go fishin in you find your swimmin-dumb soul.

Coloratura | Scalloped sootywing, california sister, ruby-spotted swallowtail, pink-edged sulphur, carolina satyr, sickle-winged skipper, sachem.

Intervallic | Take nothin with you, bring nothin back.

Not for me | Not a nightmare if it tells me what I didn't know.

Early autumn | Fine gold this first bright cold foisted on these half-buried bones. White soon but not now, not yet, these knobs, knuckles, knees. Not white quite yet, this crooked spine.

Soon | Cattails in shallow water, one tree tall among them.

Say When

Swingmatism	You hear a *bird* sing, you don't try to understand.
Sissle	Listen to anything long enough it'll tell you your life.
Tiny	Pine siskin, dickcissel, longspur, purple finch, lark sparrow, wheatear, winter wren, waterthrush, veery.
Ornithology	Bird dream felt like fell from the nest, felt like gray and wet, felt like big eyes never opened. Useless yellow beak. No cat, sure, but crows and ants and which is worse? Done nothin wrong don't matter. Felt like grass hide me but not long. Felt like fell this once never gonna fly.
How high the moon	She sparrow. He owl.
Klacktoveedsedstene	Keep flyin low over my head, them birds. I reach up finally and touch one passin by. Touch it, touch her.
Heroin	Start skitter of swifts, end leaf trapped in a sheeta ice.
Confirmation	Spectin me to answer or spectin me to sing?

Black Coffee

Desire	|	Somebody gotta ask why not.
This mood	|	Lay down step down rock trickle moss-quiet creek come down two wet-hushed hollows meet steady down fern-green downy-back leaf-rustle keep cold brier-safe mudbreasted bluebird deer-drinkin shade.
Shulie	|	Baneberry, brickelbush, bear grass, mission bells, bitterroot, bleeding heart.
All I need	|	Mmm hm. Mmm hm.
Mean to me	|	You is awful. How much you.
It never	|	Seem like songs all say I died fore I was born. Seem like singin make me happier than you.

Now's the Time

Three deuces | What's the smallest space in which I can live my life whole?

Shh | Dream the drowned city long enough you wave green and quiet and slick. Shopping carts curled off boats by beered-up boys cold to a lattice of rust. Bubble-nuzzled, scale-fondled, fin-skimmed. Last past how you know to live.

Sly | How birds pass through pickets on an unpainted fence: land feet-first on the lower rail, then lean forward to take off on the other side.

So what | My *life* is forbidden.

Nefertiti | Carry you with me. Yes you is. Yes I do.

Zouk | The way a tree sounds in wind at the edge of the world.

Boplicity | Lives of passion and scrape.

Alton | Squirrels here fraid nobody but nervous now must be comin some snow.

Sheets of Sound

Kolax	|	Some sensation sent up sell down data.
Montuna	|	Mountains rise out of song toward the god they intuit.
Cleanhead	|	Fall down showed me shouldna.
Whole tone	|	Black witch, wounded hawk, webworm, royal walnut, whistling, welsh wave, wainscot, pretty widow.
Trinkle	|	Softer than before sing warm through me wind.
A love supreme	|	Truth is I am nothing. Truth is too I could not make myself so, or see myself so by myself. I needed *it,* my nothingness. Now I hear.
Ascension	|	Cold train go slow uphill through snow. Slow uphill anyway. Wide bed fold up into wall. Ladder lean against.
Pursuance	|	If I believed I'd've tried to say plain what I said crooked. If I believed I'd've said what I sung.

The Well-Tempered Clavier

For the use and practice of young musicians who desire.

Prelude and Fugue No. 1 in C

My life makes sense the way a wildebeest's does: first weakened
by illness and thirst: then separated from the herd then
surrounded then captured: one lioness takes his neck in her
jaws: the others have his hindquarters: dust rises and the brittle
grasses give way goodbye goodbye: the wildebeest's eyes bloom
with fear and ecstasy: first he knows nothing then he feels
nothing: then his front legs buckle.

·

disbelief won't stop our speaking to you
don't wait for us to say who we are
that's the least of your worries
listen for names you might hear poison
settle at night on the grass
soak through the pads in your dog's paws
disbelief won't stop our falling in love
everything here is like it is there
except there light reflects off faces
here light shines all the way through us
there dusk has begun coming earlier
here dusk always comes earlier
disbelief won't stop our telling you lies
don't wait for love to return
it never comes back it follows us
listen for names you might hear yours
in the fog muted and diffuse
fog the atmosphere most like us
disbelief won't stop our betraying you
is that thunder we love rain
rain the weather most like us
we fall in love here again and again
things still die back to black stalk here

the rose no less than lovers' names
that it can't be never stopped love before
we fall in love here trust us trust us
our faces die back their petals brown
and fall to the poisoned grass
it's always getting dark here
it's always dusk the light most like us

Prelude and Fugue No. 2 in C minor

My cold dark salty desire: schools of krill spilled silver from light
to light: whales jailing krill in bubbles before bursting on them
from below: invisible algae and plankton suffusing the whole:
seaweed waving goodbye goodbye: jellyfish these floating
moons morsing your name here where it cannot be spoken:
sperm whale fighting squid to the death far below any light:
penguins sliding off ice into might as well be: elephant seals
swimming deeper than radio signals can sink goodbye goodbye:
orcas close to ice cruising for antarctic cod: cephalopods
signalling complex codes of color and gesture: crinoids fanning
for algae in eerie light beneath the ice: swollen tubeworms
swaying over volcanic vents: luminous fish as far below day as
stars stay above it: orcas bobbing up to peer across the ice then
sending signals with their intricate exhalations.

•

he asked me and I said no which was a half-truth
half a truth was all I had all love left me
I am myself a half-truth now whatever I was before
whatever I was when I thought I never lied
before I learned I always had lied to him and to myself
before I learned love itself is only half a truth
before I learned there are no whole truths
nothing that guileful god flaw has not fondled
of our ascertainings our words our bodies
before I knew I didn't *want* the truth
not because I couldn't bear it I can't bear what I am now
but because the me who thought she was telling the truth
also thought she could be satisfied
and this me can't bear the half-self love left me
after it asked what it asked and I said no

Prelude and Fugue No. 3 in C sharp

I lived half a life: I knew before it ended it would end this
way without malice or meaning: this pair of errant headlights
bearing down: exactly half a life: I knew I would see its end
coming: picking up speed aiming at me: half a life in all the
ways one might mean that: the other driver too drunk to choose
worn lane stripes over temptation: two bright eyes inviting this
consuming kiss: at the moment of the wreck the folding metal
told me god was her lover: who else could make my inner life
so counter to my outer: who else would have thrown me away
while he was claiming her: who else could tire of swans and
showers of gold and burning bushes: who else could come as
cancer to claim her from the inside out.

·

we are consuming you because we can because we must
we started with your breasts because he loved them so
we started there to prove we loved them even more
but then we had to prove we loved all of you
as much as he loved your every part and aspect
and after that we had to prove we loved only you
and prove we needed nothing else
if only we could have you if only we could become you
if only we could keep ourselves secret
until we were you and you us
we are consuming you because we can because we must
because it is our nature to consume and yours to be consumed
because we love you more than he does
because we love you more than anyone could
because as love in its purest form we give you your purest form
we are consuming you because we can because we must
unlike his our need for you is absolute our hunger unmitigated
he loves you and himself and other women other objects other
          dreams

our affections are undivided so we ourselves divide
suppose we stopped what then we would only prove
we were lying to you and lying to ourselves
we had to continue we have to continue
until no distinction remains between our will and yours
between your body and ours your life and ours
we are consuming you because we can because we must
we are consuming you faster than lies are consuming him
dividing faster than the will divides for fear or hunger

Prelude and Fugue No. 4 in C sharp minor

My drifting desire: continents longing for the larger selves they
lost long ago: moonlust and salt that splits them still and will
until rain finally wins its contest with rock: matching shorelines
floating slowly apart goodbye goodbye: hissing lava weeping at
the seams: earthquakes sighing over slow slow slow separation:
rift valleys gathering their inhospitable pools: flamingoes
phoenixed from the scalding waters.

●

if you were going to kiss her you should not have waited so long
if you were going to kiss her you should have fucked her
if you were going to kiss her you should have planned it
or planned it better don't lie to yourself you *did* plan it
if you were going to kiss her you should have kissed her more
        than once
you should be kissing her now why are you listening to us
if you wanted a secret life you should have kept it secret
or made it a life you soulless bastard
escape now into your body this is your last chance
don't add this to your list of failures
it will be the grain that pushes you under
the dead speak only to those who might as well be
we are helpless before our desires for ourselves
but we can make our desires for *you* come true
and they may not match your own desires
we will keep talking though not to you for long
because she will be gone and you will be with us
giving up again and again all the gifts
you always knew the universe would take back
including her especially her

Prelude and Fugue No. 5 in D

Everything turned to music in my head: my fingers followed
but not fast enough: I had no talent but I was possessed: for one
moment I gave up all I had: nothing and the illusion it was love:
everything turned to music in my head: music doesn't *have* to
live in the world: god might sell music but he doesn't give: I
had no talent I was just possessed: I saw what I doubt so often
repeated I had to *insist* on disbelief: everything turned to music
in my head: what god promised me and what he threatened
looked alike after you took your blouse off: though I had no
talent I was possessed: nothing ever *just happens* but you did:
had you not killed me I would have killed myself: everything
turned to music in my head: I had no talent but I was possessed.

•

I am the angel of buckled steel
I am the angel of long blank scratchy messages
angel of the concluding click and dial tone
of qualities of character you admire but do not possess
I am the angel of diplomacy undone
angel of surreptitious longings all longings *are* surreptitious
I am the tap and knock of cooling metal
star-bright eyes watching from the woods
crushed milk cartons cross-shredded documents
another nerve center burned beyond recall
I am your almost lover your many lovers never to be
though god himself can't name them all
I am the angel of fugitive desert flowers dormant between rains
angel of all your corrupt inclinations
and just so you'll know you will try and try the rest of your life
but you will never make her happy
you can't make her happy though you can make her sad
every decision is equally bad
original sin needs no god and you are the proof

Prelude and Fugue No. 6 in D minor

My clandestine desire: a seated woman in a lit room seen from
the street releasing her hair from a french braid and brushing it
smooth with slow strokes: her steam-heated second-floor room:
how her hair alters the name *auburn:* the tiny sparks her brush
strokes coax that would be visible if the watcher were with
her and the room dark: the sound of her brush separating the
strands goodbye goodbye: steam fighting the pipes for release:
her bare shoulders changing shape through each stroke: the
longing with which she looks into her own dark eyes.

•

the gods keep to themselves even here
we hear them yes but in whispers inscrutably
like voices in another room less heard than intuited
the gods keep to themselves everywhere
their mumbling indistinct between gusts of wind
sometimes the living are spirits too
they speak in flashes of light we see them from the corners of
      our eyes
there are no souls but there are voices
there are nights the crickets make sense
sometimes even the insects are spirits
don't try to name this voice don't try to locate it
the answer to all your questions about it is yes
is it from your wife yes is it from her lover yes
is it from your own bad conscience yes
is it from god yes of course the devil yes the devil too
is it from the dead yes from the boy you once picked a fight
      with yes
the first girl you loved yes the first you betrayed yes was she the
      same of course
from those who trusted you yes those who knew better yes
from the part of you that knew every piece of this long ago yes yes

Prelude and Fugue No. 7 in E flat

When god took back her world the instant felt like falling
backward into water: above me bubbles sizzled into light: my feet
and fingers flailed for fundament: my senses flooded with fugitive
clarity: had you not been so sudden and death so sensuous I
might have made more effort to swim: I thought I needed air
until I left it.

                •

we are less afraid than you because our fears have been confirmed
you think we will give you advice you think we care about you
we neither love by your logic nor are bound by your body
we know why you want to sleep but we also know why you can't
the stairs and floorboards speak with your weight we speak with
            your dying
fear visits only when you are dreaming but when are you not
we are less afraid than you because our fears have been confirmed
we suffer here you will too what could stop that nothing nothing
we neither love by your logic nor are bound by your body
our voices know you as bodies to your souls so words to ours
the stairs and floorboards speak with your weight we speak with
            your dying
go on keep trying to sleep it would only prove you are us
we are less afraid than you because our fears have been confirmed

Prelude and Fugue No. 8 in E flat minor

My white and ivory desire: a sheet of snow sliding slowly off a
sloped roof goodbye goodbye: origami swan swimming a lake of
lace: rice on porcelain: snow as it slopes off the eave assuming
the curve of your hips: that spring day sitting in bright sun on
stone stairs: what I know how to say to you sinking under what
I don't: snow landing on snow with a soft *oof.*

•

always and only of you
when I said god I meant you
when I said death I meant you
when I said evil
when I said your name
when I said someone else's
when I said nothing
when I said what you wanted to hear
or what you did not
when I insisted on what you had tried to deny
and admitted what I had tried to deny
when I told you the truth
when I told you lies which I did more often
when I told you something you could believe
when I told you something you couldn't
when I told you something you had to believe
though it was false and both of us knew it
and now my love especially now

Prelude and Fugue No. 9 in E

What I want has nothing to do with how I act: how I act has
nothing to do with who I am: who I am has nothing to do with
what I want: what I want haunts me an angry juvenile ghost:
invisible destructive running through the rooms: what I want
has nothing to do with how I act: I want a lot that I will never
tell about: acts and people most of whom you know by name:
who I am has nothing to do with what I want: my first death
found my second when she and I met: their single shadow our
substitute for time: what I want has nothing to do with how I
act: my desires drink and pick fights and stay out all night: I sip
tea and practice the piano at home: who I am has nothing to do
with what I want: if only my happiness were not infinite: if only
I had some respite from the sublime: that I want you I attic off
from how I act: who I am I cellar away from what I want.

•

life proved less important than I thought
though also more beautiful far more beautiful
it hurts me less than I thought it would
to have no life no touching only voices
but it grieves me more if I could weep I would
I miss tear ducts I didn't use them enough
I miss my body I didn't use it often enough
I miss my lungs they burned after a hard run on a cold morning
I miss my fingers they touched far too few hot beach rocks
even in the time of touching the time before the voices
they touched too few tautly tendoned wrists of lovers

Prelude and Fugue No. 10 in E minor

My sunburned desire: atop hot boulders lizards lying lazily across
each other: their pineal eyes that learned a hundred million years
ago to track the sun: octopi in shallow water hiding under rocks:
bright quick colors caressing the fragile reef: sand wearing itself
smooth: the long long yawns of iguanas lolling leather tongues:
shorebirds fascinated by their intermittently submerged feet:
pelicans diving and diving: gulls in flight dropping shellfish onto
rocks to break them open.

•

can a passacaglia be sung I can't remember
how does a tongue feel on the back of my neck I can't remember
or someone's fingers tracing my shoulderblades I can't remember
who is speaking here me or her or you I don't remember
does love start because it has already started it must
did I fall in love with you because I was in love already I must have
has anything harmed me more than love no nothing
how does it feel to meet another's eyes and be unable to breathe I
        can't remember
what is it like to hear your lover's voice *and* touch her body I can't
        remember
though I can still name what I miss about the old life
hiss of water in pipes the curve of a particular spine
breaking up clods of clay to mix them with peat
squirrels hanging by their back paws stretching down
to clutch clusters of maple seeds at the ends of branches
pairs of maple seeds shaped like bats handfuls of spent flowers
holding a steaming cup of tea while standing in snow
hummingbirds hummingbirds above all hummingbirds
anything that feeds on flowers and shines in the sun
and need not sing because it can fly backward
knows something the gods would keep to themselves
if there were gods

Prelude and Fugue No. 11 in F

Had we not kissed cartographers would not have mapped the
mud nor species diverged nor continents floated apart: had we
not kissed we would never have been born: our ancestors would
not have crossed the savannah through chest-high grass on their
two new legs or left the hunt-stained caves goodbye goodbye:
flowers would not have beckoned bees nor trees risen from clay
nor their leaves fallen back into it to form fossils: nor planets
wandered nor galaxies formed nor stars burned out nor nebulae
spawned lavender clouds larger than any possible human world
though no larger than our impossible one.

•

I always heard voices I thought everyone did
I can't tell you what I'm crying about though it will kill you too
the voice of the real always comes from a ghost that's the problem
if I spent less time naming my cravings at night
or knew fewer cravings to name
I might be speaking now through someone else
bringing better news and to more people
the voice of the real always comes from a ghost that's the problem
the unspared can speak to the spared
but the spared cannot speak back
the voice of the real always comes from a ghost that's the problem
this is my only voice you only listen when I'm sleeping
when you think you're hearing someone else
the voice of the real always comes from a ghost that's the problem
the real cannot speak but the rest can and does
which means that if you can speak
you are not real and it means I break the rule

Prelude and Fugue No. 12 in F minor

My parched desire: the way nomads at a drying water hole in
Mali wait for the elephants to leave: how the herd knows when
to start across the desert goodbye goodbye: their urge for the
savannah on the other side: relentless desert sun: the number
who will die during migration: lives lived water to water and
ended in between: how the dead will be consumed and by what
voracious patiences: that the others will continue: how they
know when the rains will come: that they know what will be
green beyond the sandstone ridge: how the whole herd learned
what no one elephant knows.

•

call it somaphagia we are eating your sleep
a sweet to make the devils envy us
you wouldn't listen until we started eating you
then it was too late at first we were just warning you
then we loved you and nothing is more deadly
you wouldn't listen so we started eating you
we knew before you held her hand you were going to
we knew how long your first kiss would last
we saw it before you did we know what you don't know
and never will about her and about yourself
you didn't listen when we started eating you
you thought you knew yourself everyone thinks that
but the person you knew was not you and never had been
keep trying not to listen but we have started eating you
we heard what you told her yesterday
we know what you will tell her tomorrow
we know why she believes you though you are lying
and why you think you are telling the truth when you lie to her
and how long it would take her to stop believing you
if you were going to live that long
don't listen then but now that we are eating you
we know how long it will be before you stop believing yourself

Prelude and Fugue No. 13 in F sharp

She knew before I knew: she was the one who told me: she
held my heart in her two hands and read it: my heart blue and
packed in ice and very still: her cordomancy told her and I
listened at night while the voices ate her alive: in twenty-four
keys she spoke in her sleep: with forty-eight fires Bach invented
the sun: with forty-eight outlines Shostakovich tried to trace
his own uncertain but certainly shadowed shadow: twenty-four
nights she spoke in her sleep or *he* spoke or *they* did the voices
whoever they were: I only had to cradle her head the way she
cradles hearts and they spoke: all you do she said is turn it this
way turn it that when the doctors say: focus on holding still so
they can sew: she said only holding someone else's failing heart
helped her feel her own: *they* said nothing I did not know: they
said she would die: they said I would die: they told me when
and how: in twenty-four fugues they said goodbye goodbye:
find here so many preludes more for the trunk of my car: I
wanted to see if these two dozen would burn: I knew I would: I
knew I already had.

•

I substituted love when denied happiness
I substituted loyalty when love withdrew
I substituted pretense because I had been disloyal
long ago from the start always
I substituted sullenness when I failed at pretense
I settled in the end on self-destruction
something I know now I have a talent for
as I know my name only when I see it
spelled on your irises in a code no one else knows
I know your name when I speak it the only way I can
stroking your neck with my thumb
I leave with you the name I need no longer
written on a yellow ginkgo leaf

Prelude and Fugue No. 14 in F sharp minor

My alien desire: brown broadened to green in a river delta seen
from above: salt replacing surrendered silt: barracuda in place of
piranha: ancestors buried in biers up the sides of cliffs: children
buried in the trunks of trees to be carried to heaven by their
growth: birdhouse-sized shrines built for small furtive saints and
hung in trees: infant sea turtles' ungainly race across moonlit
sand: the first turtle's feeling as a withdrawing wave lifts it into
the sea: adult turtles' ghostly floating goodbye goodbye: one
eel curled in an s mouth open motionless on brown sand and
dead coral: inland an underground river flowing through karst:
waves breaking over and over on towered lava their white foam
patiently shaping its stacked black sheets.

•

why curse desire when you must breathe it
why be content with a single voice
who would we love if not for ghosts
how will you know the lies we tell from the truths
how will you distinguish lies you want to believe from ones you
        should
will you trust the voices from nowhere enough to follow their
        commands
if not why not if so why
who would we love if not for ghosts
why are we speaking to you and why were you listening for us
so late at night why were you still awake why are you awake now
why would we *want* to understand our own words
why would our saying them make them ours
who would we love if not for ghosts
do you trust your urges your instincts your memory
do you trust your judgment do you trust the voices in your head
can you still trust what you know is leading you to death

can you follow what you distrust in preference to what you trust
or maybe that question should be the other way around
who would we love if not for ghosts
what are you listening for how will you know when you hear it
do the voices come from her dreams or our dreams or yours
what would you tell us if you knew anything
what do you wish you could tell that you can't
who do you wish you could tell it to
who would we love if not for ghosts
why is it forbidden to love more than one person
give us a good answer to *that*

Prelude and Fugue No. 15 in G

A kiss may be demonic or divine or both at once like a familiar
song: a kiss can end your life one ended mine: now I understand
original sin: no one but you ever *was* listening: a kiss may be
demonic or divine: my affections are strong my actions mean:
I did what I did instead of thinking: a kiss can change your
life one altered mine: wings folded my desires sleep upside
down then swarm out at dusk and see by singing: a kiss may be
demonic or divine: a butterfly warming itself in bright sun can
light on your hand and pulse its wings: a kiss can end your life
one ended mine: why would I live any moment again that was
not perfectly devastating: a kiss may be demonic or divine: the
kiss that gave me your life ended mine.

•

we were happier when you let me decide what lies to tell you
instead of demanding lies you thought you wanted to hear
I was never who either of us thought I was
is it love to lie and tell you so or to lie and say I'm not
in the end *everything* gets left out of the story
if I had told better lies I might have believed myself
one mouth trails another mouth through kisses through words
if this answers questions they are not the ones I asked
and certainly not the ones you think I should answer
the living ask different questions than the dead
we might have made it if you had let me lie
I might have told better lies if I had believed myself
I might still love you if you had let me not know for sure
we were happier when you let me lie to myself
decide now how honest you want me to be and about what

Prelude and Fugue No. 16 in G minor

My silver gelatin desire: arms raised praising the naked name of
napalm: a bare-shouldered man whose own biceps make him
bow: corn-stubble bowing to vacant house and vacant horizon:
backs leaving a landing boat leaning forward waist-high in
waves: schools of bullets swimming swiftly by: ten white body
bags fugitive into the sea: two white grocery bags steadfast in
front of a tank: one pacific body engulfed in its own flames.

•

we sometimes doubt your existence too
we speak with or without your listening
we keep talking what else can we do
maybe you need us worse than we need you
maybe you are no more real than we are
we sometimes doubt your existence too
you want us in your mouth to chew
but we are voices only voices
we keep talking what else can we do
if you weren't there our words would put you there
what shows you otherwise maybe they do
we sometimes doubt your existence too
to us *you* are only voices
you think they only overwhelm you
but we still feel memory and desire
these words these words are all we know to do

Prelude and Fugue No. 17 in A flat

Here is what I think when I try not to think of you: I think of
Bach in place of your bare belly: I think of the meteor shower to
remember that things burning out bring joy: of the middle term
between desire and death *that* is what I seek: I think I washed
up on shore and stand before you naked and dirty speaking in
lieu of clasping your knees: I think the heat this time of year
rises to mimic the gradual lifting away of my life: I think only
the disembodied speak only the disembodied listen: I think
elements more crucial than air surround and inhabit me: I think
the first seven victims of the world fell to your hands and three
or four of them were me: I think if souls could suffocate mine
would have long ago: and souls *can* suffocate and mine did: I
think another lost son struggles home hungry and ashamed: his
inheritance was not enough his name is me: I think everything
I know is at work destroying my life: I think the truth is
murderous and bent on killing *me:* I left my lesson early I think
you were my teacher goodbye goodbye: I think the gods created
everything but orchids which fallen angels make as gifts for
one another: I think I was better off before I knew what I was
missing.

●

I meant what I implied by saying what I said
and doing what I did after what you did
after you said what you promised you would never say
I meant you should listen with your wrists
I meant *I* should listen with your wrists
I meant you are bright light I am shattered glass
happy to be fractured if the pieces shine
I meant both of us know all we need to know
about the hummingbird in your feathered hand

Prelude and Fugue No. 18 in G sharp minor

My ancient desire: captured from an asteroid matter older than
the solar system: the constant background craving-naming of
the crows interrupted by the even older intermittent givings-up
of geese: twisted bristlecone pine clinging to a ledge: the ledge
leaning into wind: rhizome the size of a sea that was under the
first mammal's foot: hardwood kelson hosting coral.

•

you are the price of my restlessness and I am willing to pay
you are the reason my life became a life left behind
your shoulders your shoulders your knees your neck
your lips o jesus your lips the mole on your back your neck
your hands and fingers your ankles your eyes your neck
twenty years of sleep for twenty minutes of waking
and I would trade again I refuse to disown my desire
I left home knowing my judgment was impaired
knowing I loved you more than you loved me
knowing I loved you more than I valued my happiness
while we wait for rain my love the crops die and we wither
it could not have been me your arms were speaking to
but I listened and I heard what I wanted to hear
I wanted to hear what spoke through your arms
when it said truths too arrange themselves in constellations
my love for you *is* my will to death
because of you everyone after you no one
I sing of you in the narrowest possible sense
but you stand for everything else I cannot sing
I can call to you I still do I will call to you always
from here from one small impossibility away I can smell you
the sound of your voice is enough
it has to be nothing else is left me to hold
I hear you in the plants I smell you in the thunder

you have gone forever but still I listen to you
what I don't believe haunts me who I can't hold haunts me
what I held when I held you was more than you it was the spirits
what held you when I held you was more than me
it was the spirits it was all their songs

Prelude and Fugue No. 19 in A

I remember every kiss until I fell in love: the list of all I have includes nothing I desire: one kiss I take with me where it sent me to my grave: my desires fit my life like a second right-hand glove: the soul generates light only at its departure: I remember every kiss until I fell in love: once I wanted happiness I *wanted* to believe: now I find I much prefer the solace of despair: the kiss I carry with me sent me to my grave: anything intense enough to feel is fugitive: nothing I want lasts long enough to name or declare: I remembered every kiss after I fell in love: you are my failure to conceal everything I crave: till you showed me I didn't know I was what we are: the kiss no one can take away sent me to my grave: even if I *could* remain intact I wouldn't have: I had looked for myself before and found nothing there: I remember every kiss as your one kiss my love: the kiss I carry with me still here in my grave.

•

yes to all your questions yes to those you do not ask
yes no matter what the answer ought to be
yes I love you yes of course no not more than I love her
yes you can love two people but one won't want to know
yes there are laws but no one tells us either
yes I stopped speaking your name out loud
no I did not stop *repeating* your name
I can't keep it secret so I say it to myself
yes this is what love becomes
infinite distance and endlessly repeating your name
yes you made me suffer then yes I suffer still
yes I want to suffer more if it means you

Prelude and Fugue No. 20 in A minor

My winter-dented desire: blacktop broken off the road in
chunks: the road laid down too near the shore cracked and
sinking: the same sunken road seen through leaning trees: rain-
dark mulch pock-marked where squirrels dug up bulbs: hollow
places creatures find to hibernate: the flowered places far away
to which they fly: wet leaves under snow hosting mold: one
lone leaf caught in a cobweb between a window and its shutter.

•

I know what you want I had your desires
I *became* your desires that is my hell
you want another life more lives
with more lovers and you will get those lives
you are getting them now without knowing it
more lives all as empty and unknowing as this one
all as drained by unfulfilled desire
each beautiful and generous lover
shadowed by another you cannot have
your desires are my hell and mine yours
you may love as much as you want
but have none of what you love
first I sank in water then I sank in light

Prelude and Fugue No. 21 in B flat

I cannot see you from here: I can draw no closer but love I smell
you still: I kiss you in the only way I can: the way we kiss who
cannot kiss: who bloom but briefly: who make as make we must
bright fertile colors of our muddy yearnings: I kiss you with
sheer wings and six pollen-laden legs: I send you another bee.

 •

time here is a function of the voice
here your voice is not *your* voice
sleep is a function of the voice
sleep itself speaks and others speak through it
your voice here is a function of the spirit
it is not *you* anymore afterward not anyone
we are no one in particular certainly not you
we are inseparable indistinguishable
we are your lover and your husband alike
we do not distinguish as you do
even between the dead and the living
so we speak to you from beyond
but we are also some of those
who are not yet beyond as you see things
though you will see as we see soon enough

Prelude and Fugue No. 22 in B flat minor

My saurian desire: sensory cells that dot my jaw and detect even
tiny vibrations: a valve at the back of my throat to keep out
water: mirrors behind my eyes to double light at night: my urge
to carry my young to the water in my mouth after they hatch:
the ability to hold my breath underwater and lie at the bottom
motionless for hours waiting for prey: my tiny tiny brain that
knows only hunger but knows it well: the months one meal can
last me: my instinct to roll so that I twist off whatever limb my
jaws have clutched: the 240 million years that make mine the
oldest hunger.

•

when I die let them find me in your arms
when your arms found me I was dying already
I started dying when I became yours
in your arms I died again and again
I was yours long before you found me
when I die let them find me in your arms
I speak to you now that I am dead
from the beginning your arms spoke to me
I started dying when I became yours
I answered one death with another
I taste you still though I no longer see
when I die let them find me in your arms
now in my death I speak of your arms
if I die in your arms let no one find me
I started dying when I became yours
you found me because I was dying
I became yours because I was dying
when I die let them find me in your arms
I started dying when I became yours

Prelude and Fugue No. 23 in B

After the crash I plan to be the god of symmetry and silhouette:
of the light bright between your legs: of dusk on the hill behind
another mona lisa: of the scurfed skin on a turtle's neck: after
the wreck I aim to be the god who makes your irises who sets
in those two circles six hundred glacial lakes seen from the sky:
after the crash after I can no longer listen let someone else:
I plan at last to have a voice of my own in the next world a
brighter world than this one but still made of clay.

•

we are voices it is our work to send you careening
from consciousness to consciousness like tumbling down a hill
voices do not need motive and cause
one thing following from another is your idea not ours
we speak and you insist on moving your lips
naming all we have given up will take us forever
bring bundles bring baskets bowls we are hungry
if we lose touch keep on without us
how will you know which of our night visits is the last
do you want to know or would it be better not to
we speak like bleeding you go pale
and have to find a way to stop it or you die
your body *is* your soul it *will* die
we are not souls we are voices
nothing else is left us but our hunger
you think hunger comes from your body
that at least you will be released from it when you die
but hunger will remain always it is your voice it is you
it's not that we're damned no one is damned
but some lose their voice and others never had one
because we speak through someone asleep
you wonder if we tell the truth
but why not take it as a sign that we do

Prelude and Fugue No. 24 in B minor

Had I lived my cursive would have reverted to print: my capitals
to lower case: had I lived she would have left me: she always
liked me better dead: had I lived the river would have taken
longer to find its fated sea: had the swollen creek I thought I
could cross not swept me away I might have seen the doe in
her seclusion giving birth I might have found her fawn: I might
have stood in the woods and heard the breeze advancing tree
by tree: had the horse I thought I could break not thrown me
I might have made it across the plains: I might not have been
caught by the grass fires: had the squall not surprised me so
far from shore I might have watched the waves from safety
instead of sinking under them: as it is the depth of the blue here
compensates for the pressure and the cold.

•

love you or inhabit you you know which one I chose
it still counts as a secret if I say it only to the living
I believed *everything* except the voices now I am one
I feared voices from another world but I became what I feared
I regret that I did not do what I wanted to do when I wanted to
          do it
that I did not know sooner you wanted to destroy your life
as badly as I wanted to destroy mine
and you wanted *me* to destroy it
I would have tried believe me I would have tried
you should have ruined me half a life ago
maybe I knew you then maybe you destroyed my life before it
          began
I regret my past virtues I renounce them all though now it is
          too late
now I think always and only of my vices
you were one and I want more

I did not speak until you started listening
the others speak all the time but I have been waiting for you
speaking only to speak your name
your name that I say over and over
your name that I carry your name that carries me

Books from Etruscan Press

The Confessions of Doc Williams & Other Poems
  by William Heyen

Art into Life by Frederick R. Karl

Shadows of Houses by H. L. Hix

The White Horse: A Columbian Journey by Diane Thiel

Wild and Whirling Words: A Poetic Conversation
  by H. L. Hix

Shoah Train by William Heyen

Crow Man by Tom Bailey

As Easy As Lying: Essays on Poetry by H. L. Hix

Cinder by Bruce Bond

Free Concert: New and Selected Poems by Milton Kessler

September 11, 2001: American Writers Respond
  edited by William Heyen

etruscan press

Etruscan Press books may be ordered from:

Small Press Distribution
1-800-869-7553
www.spdbooks.org

Bookmasters, Inc.
1-800-537-6727
www.bookmasters.com